COLORING BOOKS
FOR ADULTS
RELAXATION

Butterflies & Mandalas

Preview of Coloring Pages

www.arttherapycoloring.com

Preview of Coloring Pages

Drawings

Best Selling Art Therapy Coloring Books

Coloring Books For Adults:

- Zombie Coloring Book: Black Background
- Butterfly Coloring Book For Adults: Black Background
- Tattoo Coloring Book: Black Background
- Coloring Books for Adults Relaxation: Native American Inspired Designs
- Fishing Coloring Book for Adults: Black Background

Coloring Books For Men:

- Coloring Book for Men: Anti-Stress Designs Vol 1
- Coloring Book For Men: Fishing Designs
- Coloring Book For Men: Tattoo Designs
- Coloring Books for Men: Hunting
- Coloring Book For Men: Biker Designs

Coloring Books For Seniors:

- Coloring Book For Seniors: Nature Designs Vol 1
- Coloring Book For Seniors: Anti-Stress Designs Vol 1
- Coloring Books for Seniors: Relaxing Designs
- Coloring Book For Seniors: Floral Designs Vol 1
- Coloring Book For Seniors: Ocean Designs Vol 1

Coloring Books For Teens and Tweens:

- Coloring Books For Teens: Ocean Designs
- Coloring Books for Teen Girls Vol 1
- Teen Inspirational Coloring Books
- Coloring Book for Teens: Anti-Stress Designs Vol 1
- Tween Coloring Books For Girls: Cute Animals

Coloring Books For Kids:

- Horse Coloring Book For Girls
- Coloring Books For Boys: Sharks
- Coloring Books for Boys: Animal Designs
- Unicorn Coloring Book for Girls
- Detailed Coloring Books For Kids

Art Therapy Coloring Books

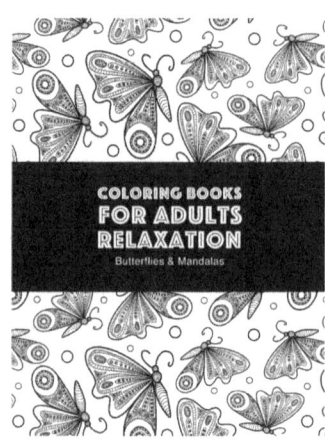

Art Therapy Coloring Books

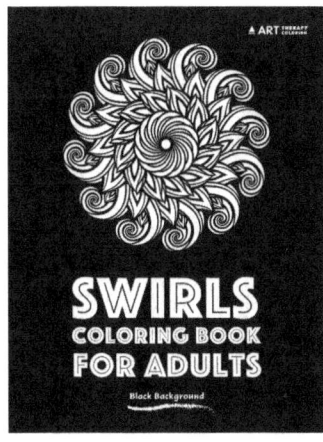

SWIRLS
COLORING BOOK
FOR ADULTS
Black Background

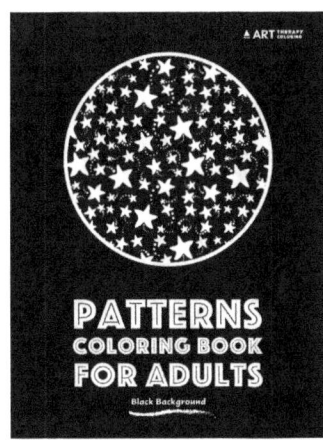

PATTERNS
COLORING BOOK
FOR ADULTS
Black Background

DRAGON
COLORING BOOK

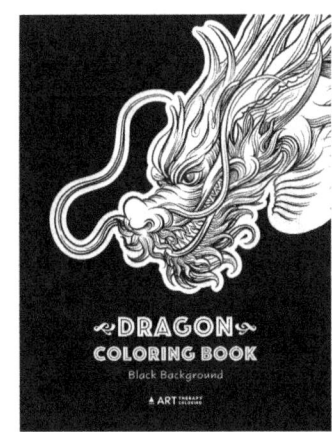

DRAGON
COLORING BOOK
Black Background

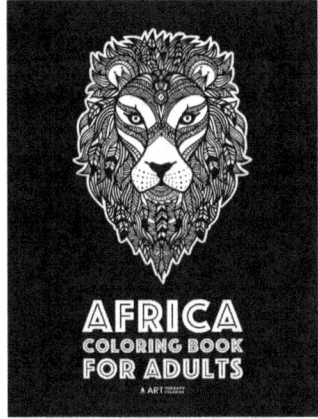

AFRICA
COLORING BOOK
FOR ADULTS

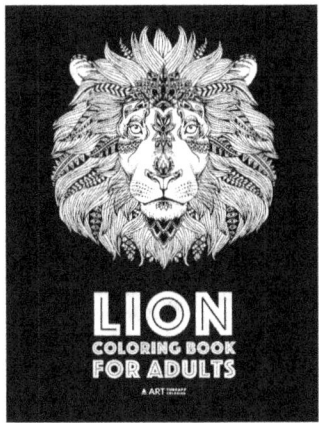

LION
COLORING BOOK
FOR ADULTS

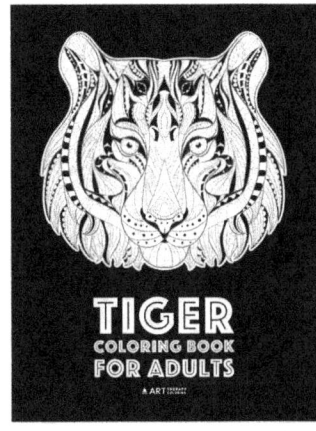

TIGER
COLORING BOOK
FOR ADULTS

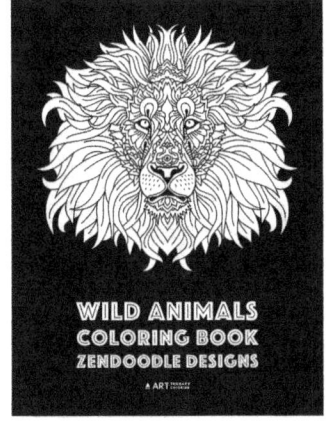

WILD ANIMALS
COLORING BOOK
ZENDOODLE DESIGNS

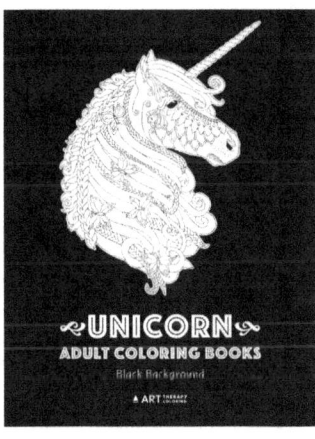

UNICORN
ADULT COLORING BOOKS
Black Background

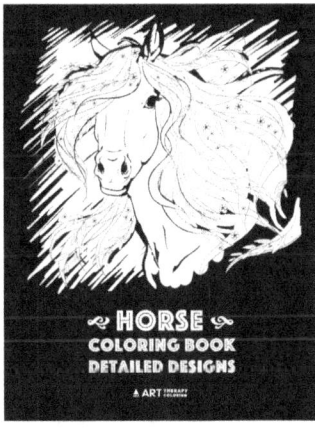

HORSE
COLORING BOOK
DETAILED DESIGNS

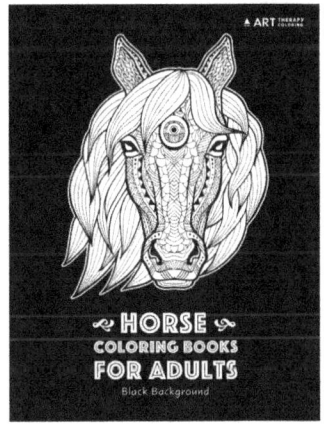

HORSE
COLORING BOOKS
FOR ADULTS
Black Background

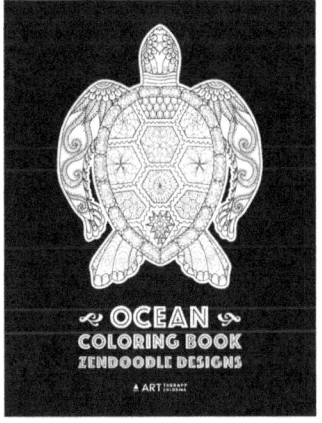

OCEAN
COLORING BOOK
ZENDOODLE DESIGNS

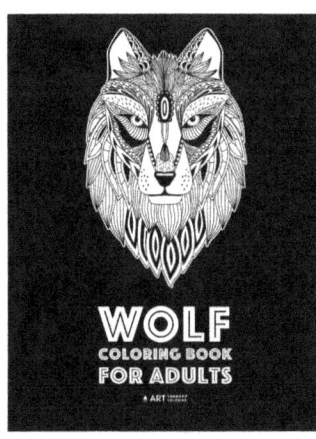

WOLF
COLORING BOOK
FOR ADULTS

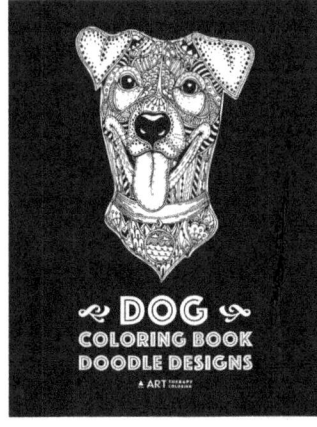

DOG
COLORING BOOK
DOODLE DESIGNS

CUTE ANIMAL
COLORING BOOK

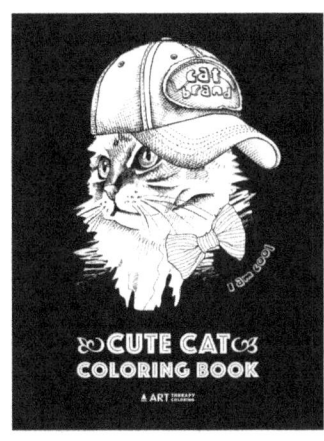

CUTE CAT
COLORING BOOK

Art Therapy Coloring Books

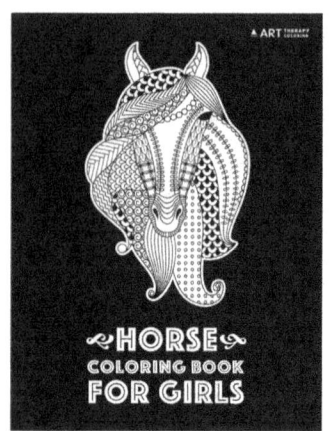

HORSE COLORING BOOK **FOR GIRLS**

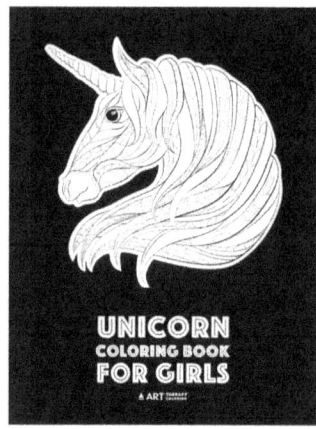

UNICORN COLORING BOOK **FOR GIRLS**

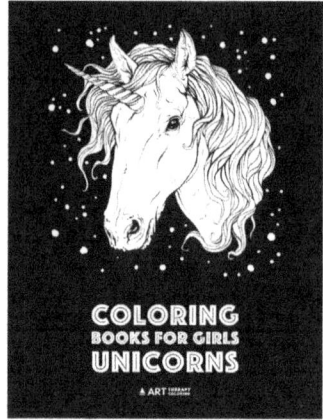

COLORING BOOKS FOR GIRLS **UNICORNS**

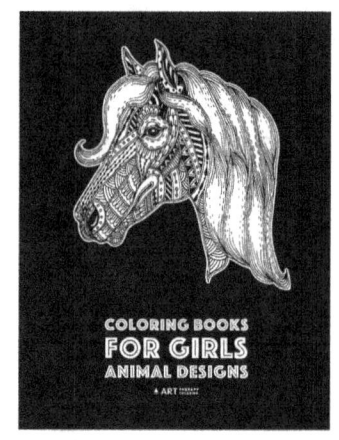

COLORING BOOKS **FOR GIRLS** ANIMAL DESIGNS

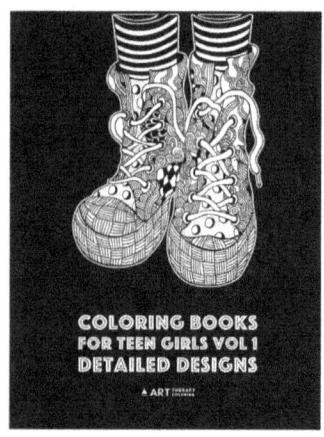

COLORING BOOKS FOR TEEN GIRLS VOL 1 **DETAILED DESIGNS**

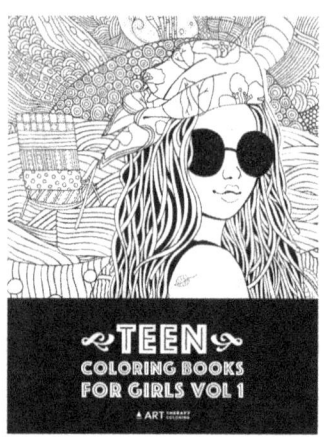

TEEN COLORING BOOKS **FOR GIRLS VOL 1**

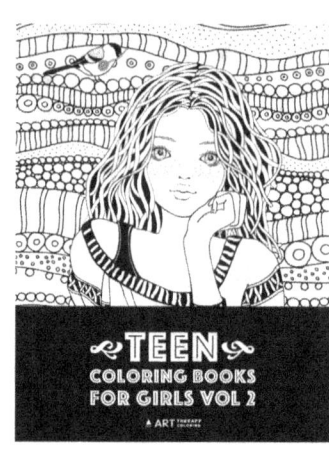

TEEN COLORING BOOKS **FOR GIRLS VOL 2**

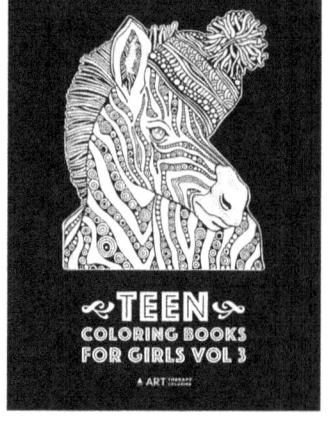

TEEN COLORING BOOKS **FOR GIRLS VOL 3**

COLORING BOOKS FOR GIRLS **CUTE ANIMALS**

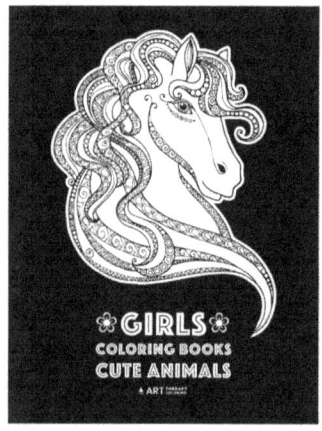

GIRLS COLORING BOOKS **CUTE ANIMALS**

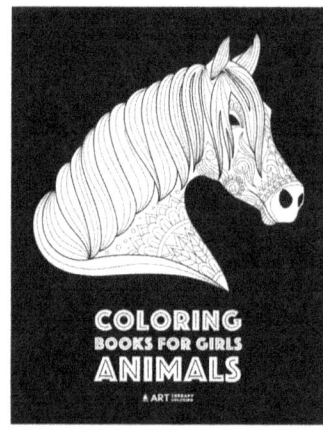

COLORING BOOKS FOR GIRLS **ANIMALS**

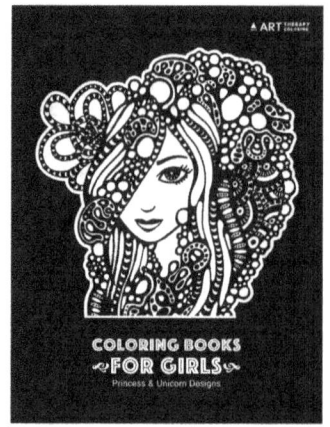

COLORING BOOKS **FOR GIRLS** Princess & Unicorn Designs

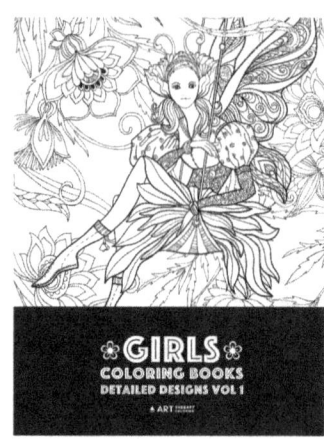

GIRLS COLORING BOOKS **DETAILED DESIGNS VOL 1**

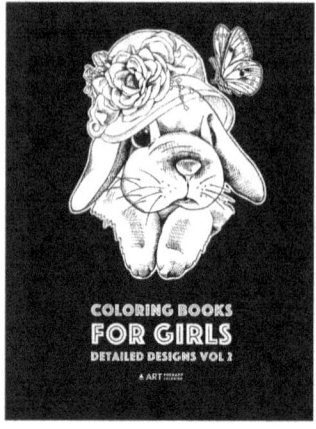

COLORING BOOKS **FOR GIRLS** DETAILED DESIGNS VOL 2

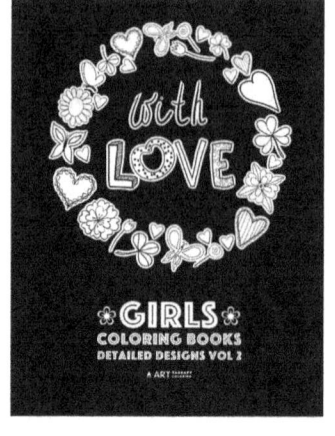

with **LOVE**

GIRLS COLORING BOOKS **DETAILED DESIGNS VOL 2**

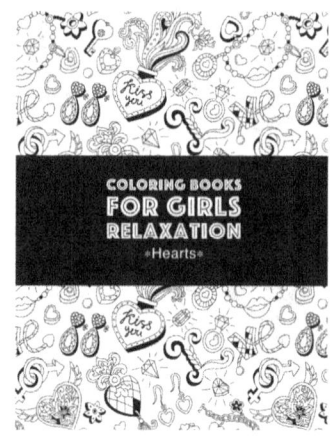

COLORING BOOKS **FOR GIRLS** RELAXATION Hearts

Art Therapy Coloring Books

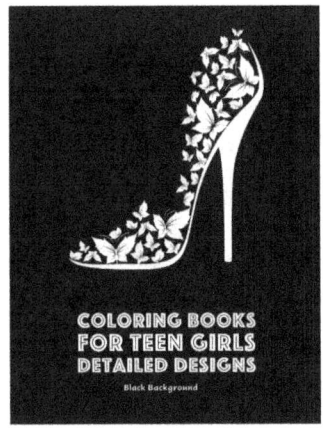

COLORING BOOKS
FOR TEEN GIRLS
DETAILED DESIGNS
Black Background

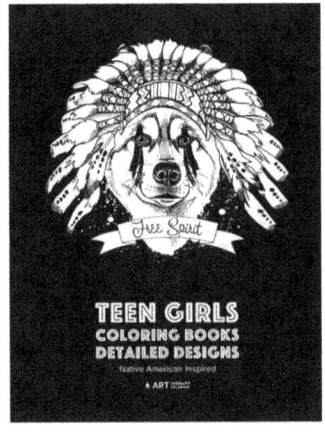

TEEN GIRLS
COLORING BOOKS
DETAILED DESIGNS
Native American Inspired

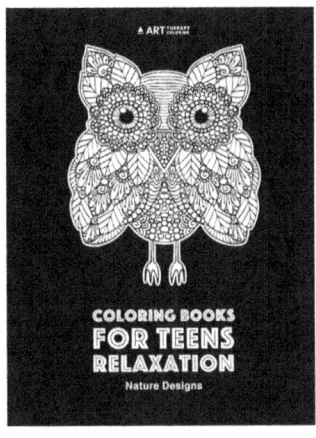

COLORING BOOKS
FOR TEENS
RELAXATION
Nature Designs

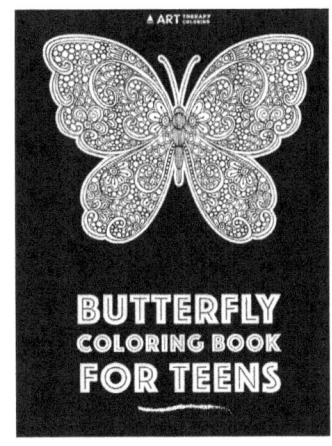

BUTTERFLY
COLORING BOOK
FOR TEENS

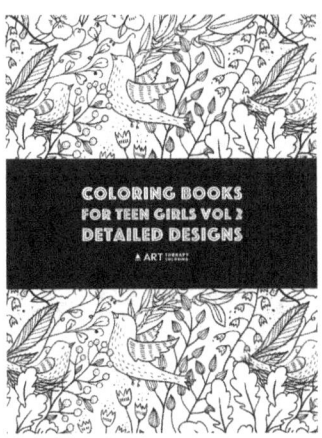

COLORING BOOKS
FOR TEEN GIRLS VOL 2
DETAILED DESIGNS

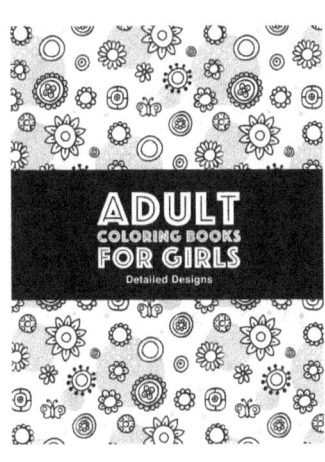

ADULT
COLORING BOOKS
FOR GIRLS
Detailed Designs

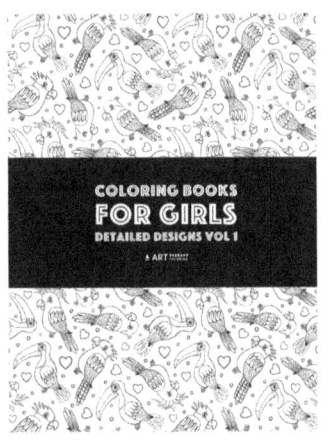

COLORING BOOKS
FOR GIRLS
DETAILED DESIGNS VOL 1

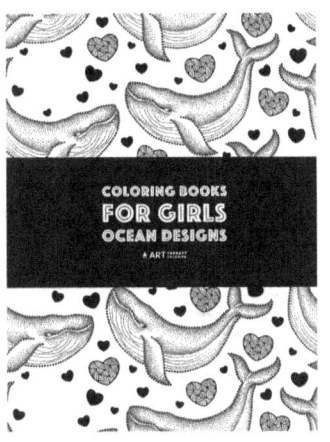

COLORING BOOKS
FOR GIRLS
OCEAN DESIGNS

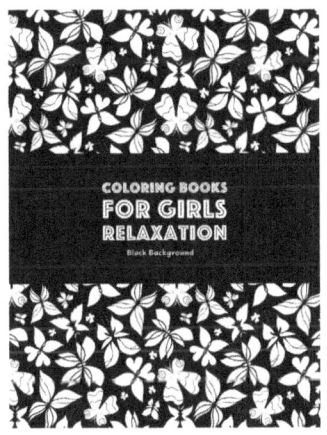

COLORING BOOKS
FOR GIRLS
RELAXATION
Black Background

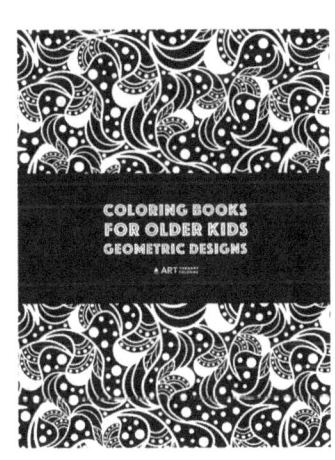

COLORING BOOKS
FOR OLDER KIDS
GEOMETRIC DESIGNS

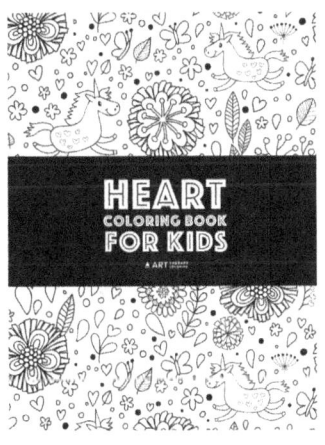

HEART
COLORING BOOK
FOR KIDS

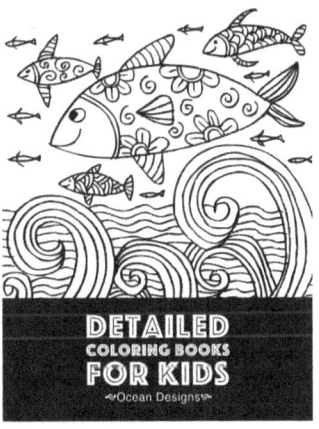

DETAILED
COLORING BOOKS
FOR KIDS
Ocean Designs

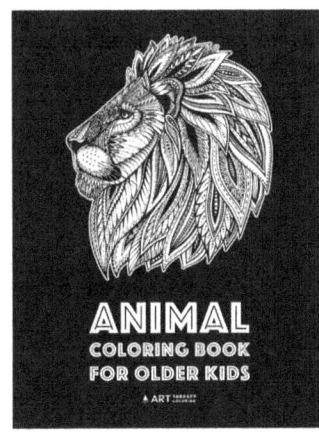

ANIMAL
COLORING BOOK
FOR OLDER KIDS

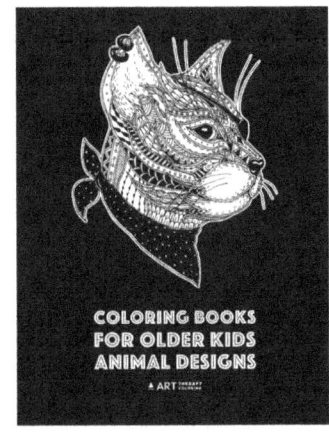

COLORING BOOKS
FOR OLDER KIDS
ANIMAL DESIGNS

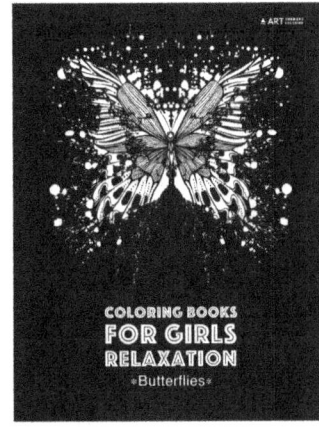

COLORING BOOKS
FOR GIRLS
RELAXATION
Butterflies

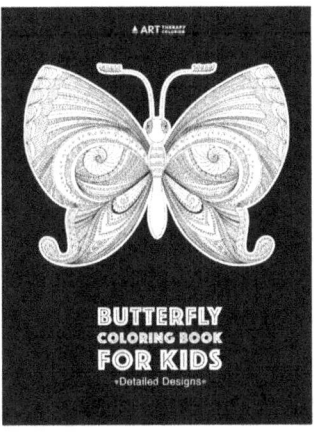

BUTTERFLY
COLORING BOOK
FOR KIDS
Detailed Designs

Art Therapy Coloring Books

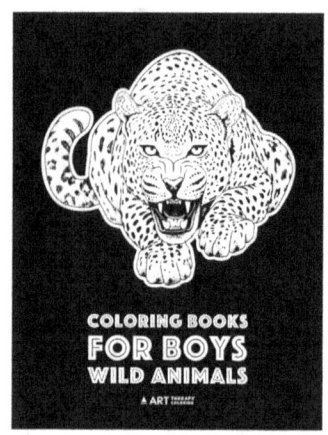

COLORING BOOKS FOR BOYS WILD ANIMALS

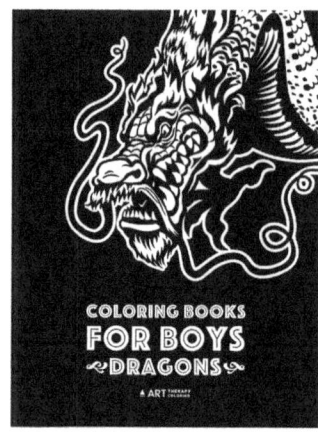

COLORING BOOKS FOR BOYS DRAGONS

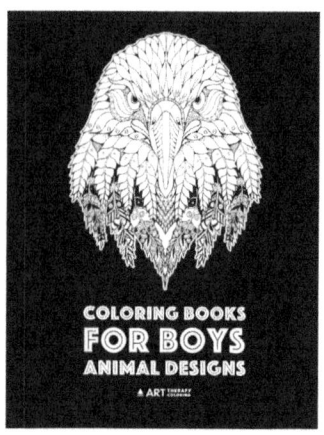

COLORING BOOKS FOR BOYS ANIMAL DESIGNS

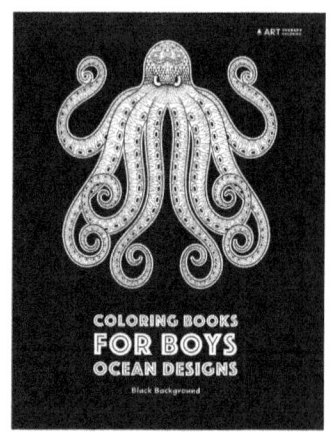

COLORING BOOKS FOR BOYS OCEAN DESIGNS
Black Background

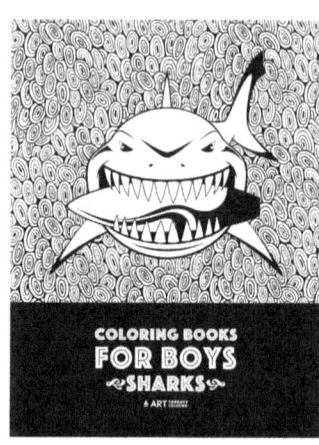

COLORING BOOKS FOR BOYS SHARKS

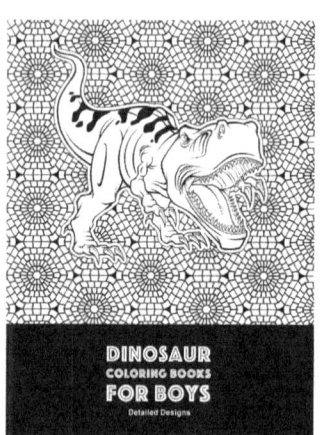

DINOSAUR COLORING BOOKS FOR BOYS
Detailed Designs

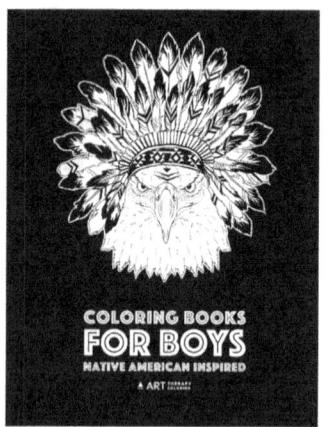

COLORING BOOKS FOR BOYS NATIVE AMERICAN INSPIRED

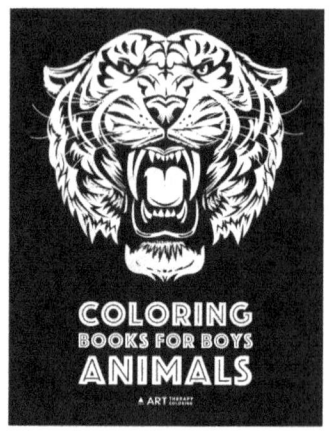

COLORING BOOKS FOR BOYS ANIMALS

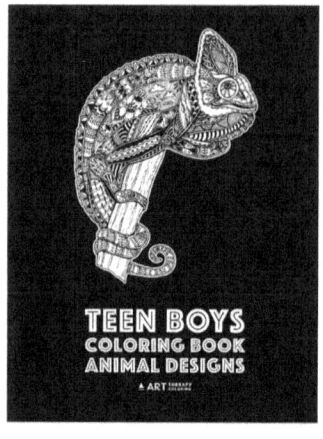

TEEN BOYS COLORING BOOK ANIMAL DESIGNS

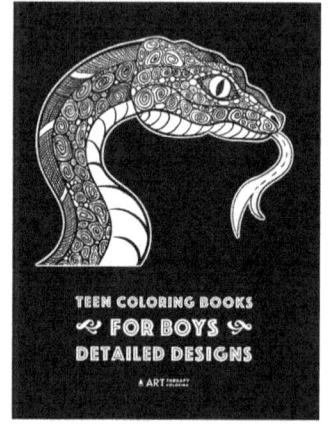

TEEN COLORING BOOKS FOR BOYS DETAILED DESIGNS

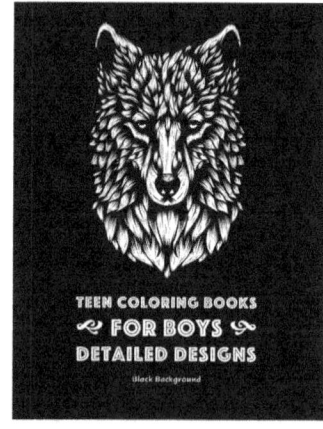

TEEN COLORING BOOKS FOR BOYS DETAILED DESIGNS
Black Background

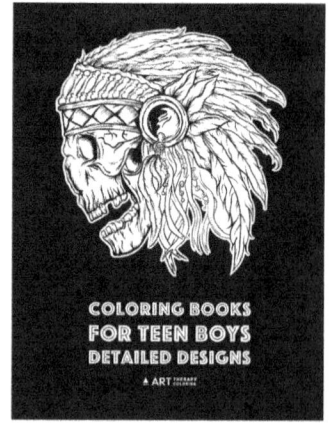

COLORING BOOKS FOR TEEN BOYS DETAILED DESIGNS

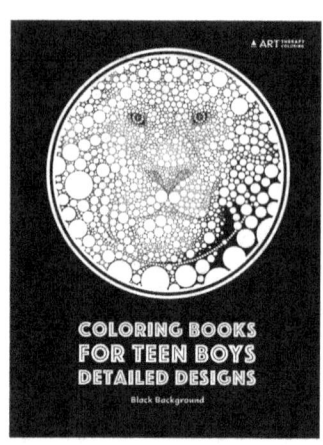

COLORING BOOKS FOR TEEN BOYS DETAILED DESIGNS
Black Background

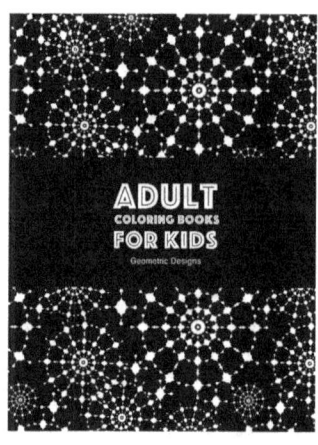

ADULT COLORING BOOKS FOR KIDS
Geometric Designs

ROBOT COLORING BOOK DETAILED DESIGNS

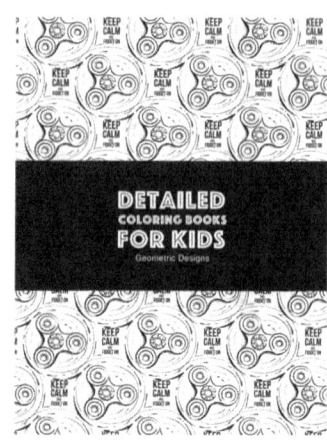

DETAILED COLORING BOOKS FOR KIDS
Geometric Designs

Art Therapy Coloring Books

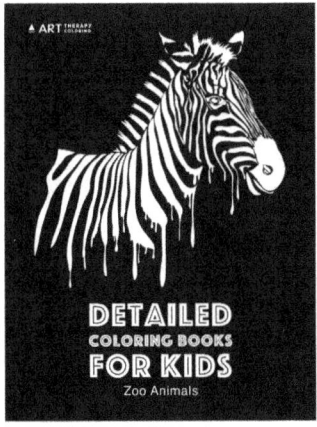

DETAILED
COLORING BOOKS
FOR KIDS
Zoo Animals

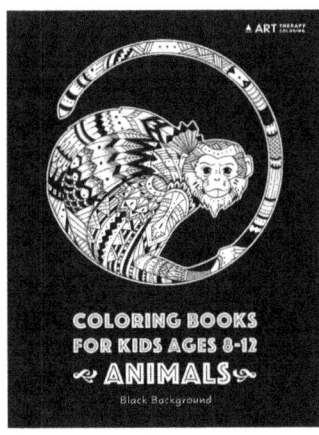

COLORING BOOKS
FOR KIDS AGES 8-12
ANIMALS
Black Background

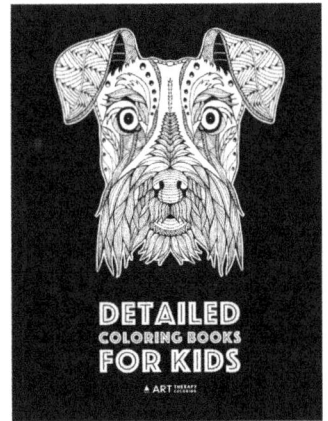

DETAILED
COLORING BOOKS
FOR KIDS

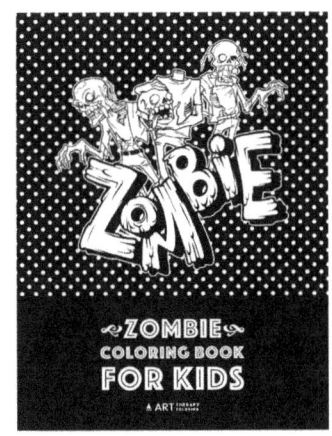

ZOMBIE
COLORING BOOK
FOR KIDS

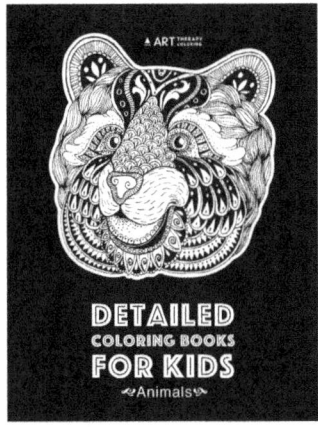

DETAILED
COLORING BOOKS
FOR KIDS
Animals

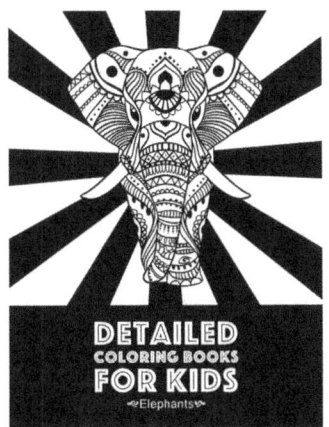

DETAILED
COLORING BOOKS
FOR KIDS
Elephants

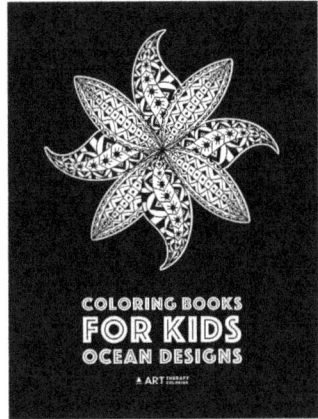

COLORING BOOKS
FOR KIDS
OCEAN DESIGNS

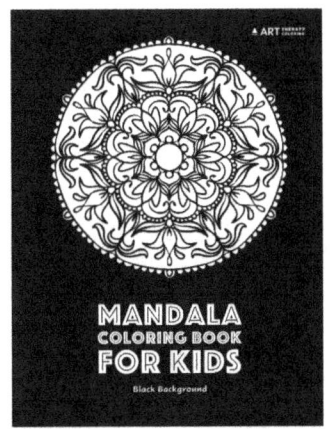

MANDALA
COLORING BOOK
FOR KIDS
Black Background

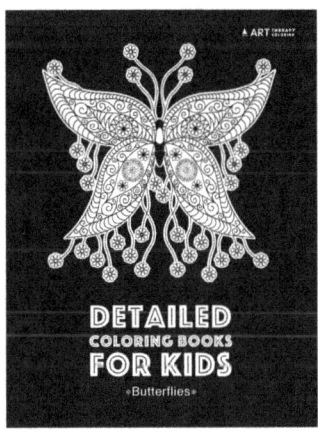

DETAILED
COLORING BOOKS
FOR KIDS
Butterflies

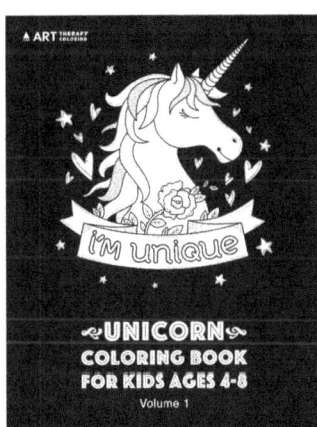

UNICORN
COLORING BOOK
FOR KIDS AGES 4-8
Volume 1

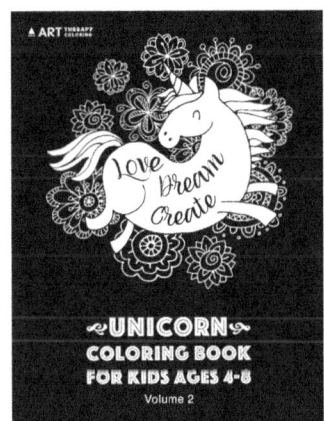

UNICORN
COLORING BOOK
FOR KIDS AGES 4-8
Volume 2

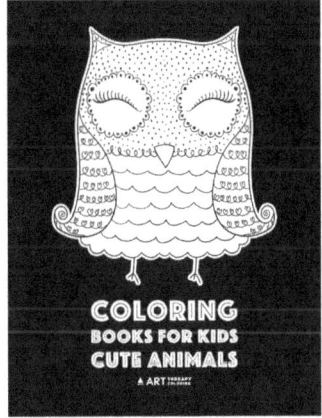

COLORING
BOOKS FOR KIDS
CUTE ANIMALS

KIDS
MANDALA
COLORING BOOK

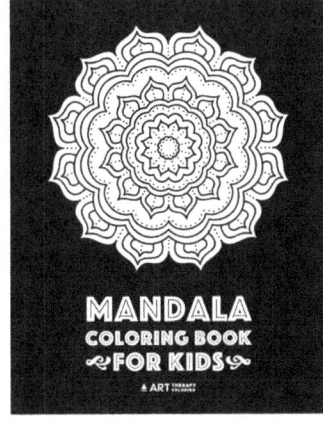

MANDALA
COLORING BOOK
FOR KIDS

SHARK
COLORING BOOK

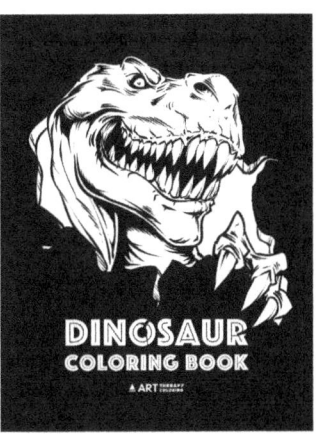

DINOSAUR
COLORING BOOK

Coloring Books For Adults Relaxation
Butterflies & Mandalas

Published by:
Art Therapy Coloring
www.arttherapycoloring.com

Shutterstock Images

ISBN: 978-1-64126-066-4

www.ingramcontent.com/pod-product-compliance
Lightning Source LLC
Chambersburg PA
CBHW081343180526

45171CB00006B/594